WHAT COULD IT BE?

Written by Jennifer Jacobson
Illustrated by Richard Bernal

HARCOURT BRACE & COMPANY

Orlando   Atlanta   Austin   Boston   San Francisco   Chicago   Dallas   New York
Toronto   London

What could it be?

2

A snake?

Not a snake.

A bird?

Not a bird.

A bear?

Not a bear!